Everyday Green Smoothies: 70 Simple and Tasty Recipes to Lose Weight, Boost Energy, and Well-Being + 7 Day Detox Plan

Julia Patel

Published by Julia Patel, 2021.

Table of Contents

INTRODUCTION

Are you want to change your life from now? Have you decided to take off extra pounds or to stick with a healthier lifestyle? Therefore, the simple green smoothie cleanse plan can help you achieve your goals.

You know that the main reason for difficulty losing weight is that there are many toxins in your body. Those toxins are stored in fat, and until you eliminate them, it is difficult to burn off extra fat.

THE GREEN SMOOTHIE detox is a simple way to tidy up the body and maintain a healthy lifestyle. This diet plan can help your body to eliminate toxins, preparing your body for weight loss safely. You can lose weight in the 7-10 days that you follow the green smoothie cleanse. Besides, most people will find that they enjoy the delicious green smoothie recipes they consume during the cleanse. This means that you can continue to use the proposed recipes for green smoothies in your daily diet.

In this book, you will find everything you need to start the green smoothie cleanse plan safely. You will find helpful information about a green smoothie, look at the main benefits, and tips for getting started with this cleanse plan.

The recipe book is packed with green smoothie recipes for every day. You will also find a simple 7-day eating plan that will help you plan your meals during the cleanse.

CHAPTER 1: ABOUT GREEN SMOOTHIES

Green smoothies are the simplest way to body detoxification, as they can be modified for a short duration and they can be modified to a life-long diet.

GREEN SMOOTHIES ARE simply the combination of a healthy range of green vegetables, fruits, and water. Of course, there are other ingredients added to the green smoothie recipe, but the major items are green vegetables, fruits, and water.

When the green smoothie is done right, it is a perfect way to detoxify the body and to lose weight. Yes! You can even lose up to 8-10 pounds!

The green smoothie is water-based and contains organic ingredients, both of which are very crucial in increasing the body's metabolism. Think of it as a quick way to ingest many green vegetables all at once. With an appropriate schedule, you can arrange the green smoothie into a diet that works for weight loss. Before we begin, you should know the benefits of green smoothie.

MAIN BENEFITS OF GREEN SMOOTHIES

There are actually many benefits to making a habit out of drinking green smoothies.

Benefit 1 – Safely Weight Loss

One of the main benefits of a green smoothie detox is safely weight loss. Even though the smoothies fill you up, the smoothies will help you lose weight, because the green smoothies are packed with low calorie green leafy veggies as a base. They have plenty of fiber in them, which will make you feel full fast.

Benefit 2 – Gentle Cleansing of Toxins

The green smoothie cleanse helps the body to eliminate toxins and waste. This helps reduce the strain of the toxic load on your body in short time and you will notice that you begin feeling better. Many of the symptoms of a high toxic load, such as headaches, fatigue and constipation will go away once those toxins are eliminated with green smoothies.

Benefit 3 – Health Improvement

The green smoothies can help you look and feel young and healthy. All the nutrients found in the raw fruits and veggies improve the function of your body and help to improve your health. After detoxing, you will notice that your skin will looking younger and healthier. All the antioxidants in the green smoothies will also help to reverse and prevent aging, reducing problems with age spots and wrinkles. As a result, you will get the healthy glowing clean skin.

Benefit 4 – Hydrate the Body

Since most functions of our body rely on water, dehydration can result in serious health problems. Since green smoothies have such a high water content, they help to dehydrate the body to improve all bodily functions. When your body is well hydrated, your immune system, brain, digestive system, muscles and other functions will work the way they should.

Benefit 5 – Improves Function of the Digestive System

The green smoothie cleanse plan will help you to improve the function of your digestive system. The digestive system does not need to work hard to digest green smoothies, since they are already in liquid form. As a result, the body can easily get the nutrients it needs from fruits and veggies. If you have some digestive problems, such as acid reflux, colitis, heartburn or irritable bowel syndrome, you may find that drinking green smoothies helps treat these problems.

Benefit 6 – Intake of Important Nutrients

The green smoothies help to increase your intake of important nutrients. Since the veggies and fruits in the smoothies are raw, they offer you more nutrients than cooked one. The green smoothies are packed with important antioxidants, vitamins, fiber, phytonutrients, minerals and more. When fruits and veggies are turned into smoothies, it makes it easier to get more fruits and veggies in your diet, improving your intake of the important nutrients.

Benefit 7 – Delicious and Easy to Prepare Recipes

Preparing the green smoothies is a breeze and takes a few minutes to prepare. With so many tasty greens and delicious fruits and veggies available, you will find so many delicious recipes to try. In fact, you can start experimenting with your own recipes.

HOW TO MAKE GREEN SMOOTHIES?

Green Smoothies are quick and easy to make. When you start off with the right basic steps, you can eventually make your own smoothie recipes.

1. CHOOSE ONE LIQUID Base

It is necessary to help your blender in mixing up all ingredients. You can make use water, coconut water, fruit juices, almond milk, green tea, or mate as a liquid base. The less liquid base you use, the thicker your smoothie will become.

2. Add Base Fruit and Berries

It will give your smoothie with creamy texture. You may use creamy and flavored fruits and berries, such as banana, papaya, mango, peach, pear, apple, kiwi, pineapple, orange, avocado, Strawberry, raspberries, blueberry, blackberry, and others.

3. Add Flavors

Add your favorite spices and flavors for a richer green smoothie flavor to kick-start your weight loss journey. Vanilla bean, clove, cinnamon, lemon, ginger, and even cayenne pepper may also be added to complement fruit flavors.

4. Add Greens

Greens taste bitter when eaten alone but when added to base fruits and flavor fruits, fruits mask out the taste of the greens.

5. Blend Fruits and Greens

All ingredients blend for 30-60 seconds until your smoothie turns bright or dark green. Caution not to over-blend your smoothie as this will lessen the nutrient content and increase oxidation.

6. Use Additives

In green smoothie preparing process, you may use different additives, such as protein powders, green powders, super foods, omega-3s, and sweeteners.

WHAT GREENS TO USE FOR GREEN SMOOTHIES?

Greens are the main ingredient of green smoothies, since they are packed with important nutrients, fiber and water. Here are some of the best greens you can use in your green smoothie recipes.

Spinach

This is one of the most well-known and well-liked dark leafy green veggies, which are often used in many green smoothie recipes. Spinach has a mild taste, which is why it is such a great ingredient to use in your smoothies. It offers many nutrients, including vitamins K, A, E and C, magnesium, omega-3 fatty acids and calcium.

Kale

Is another popular green leafy veggie, tastes wonderful with green smoothies. The delicate leaves are packed with vitamin K, C and A. Well-known, that the kale can help to reduce the risk of certain types of cancers.

Arugula

Arugula leaves are excellent for brain and bone health. Besides, they offer important nutrients, including vitamins K, C, A and folic acid.

Lettuce

Many types of lettuce exist and for your green smoothies, it is best to choose dark green lettuce leaves. Romaine lettuce is the most popular type of lettuce used for the green smoothie diet, since it contains folic acid and vitamins K, A and C.

Chard

It has a nice texture and taste. It is an excellent choice in green smoothies because it helps to clean out your digestive system and prevent the development of certain cancers.

Turnip Greens

While turnip greens have plenty of flavor, they have a bitter taste, so you would like to pair them with some sweet fruits. Turnip Green offers great healthy benefits, including helping to fight cancer.

Beet Greens

It helps to give the immune system a boost, improve vision and prevent Alzheimer's disease. It is also an excellent source of vitamin K.

Parsley

It packs a great nutritional punch, because it is packed with plenty of fiber, minerals, vitamins and antioxidants. The antioxidants fight the signs of aging and keep blood sugar levels stable.

Bok Choy

It is crunched and has a milk taste. The antioxidants, calcium and vitamin content make it an excellent addition to green smoothies.

WHAT OTHER INGREDIENTS MAY TO USE FOR GREEN SMOOTHIES?

While green leafy veggies and greens are the base of green smoothies, you can include many other foods in your smoothies as well. Adding other ingredients can help you to improve the flavor and the nutrient content of your smoothies. Let us see what other ingredients you can add to smoothies.

Fruits

They help to improve the taste of green smoothies. Many of the best green smoothie recipes call for various fruits, which also pack in many important nutrients for your body. Fruits to add to your smoothies include, but are not limited to, the following:

- Pineapple
- Mango
- Blueberries
- Apples
- Raspberries
- Strawberries
- Bananas
- Lemons
- Cherries
- Limes
- Cranberries
- Kiwi
- Papaya
- Grapes
- Peaches

Sweeteners

Natural sweeteners can be added to green smoothies if necessary, but it is best to leave them out if possible. You can add maple syrup, stevia, agave syrup as sweeteners.

Water

Purified water can be added to smoothies. It helps improve hydration and can be used to thin out the texture of your smoothies. Better, to use purified or spring water is important.

Protein

If you are working out or need some extra energy to your day, you can add protein to your green smoothies. Adding protein to your smoothies is especially important if you are planning to work out after drinking your smoothie.

Veggies

You can also add other veggies to your smoothies.

- Cucumbers
- Tomatoes
- Zucchini
- Celery
- And other veggies

GREEN SMOOTHIE DIET FOR WEIGHT LOSS

A cleansing 7-day period can be very effective only if you decide to discipline your body to go through this detoxification. This might be hard, especially the first three days are usually the most difficult because your body is adjusting to the new eating habits, but the results will be worth it.

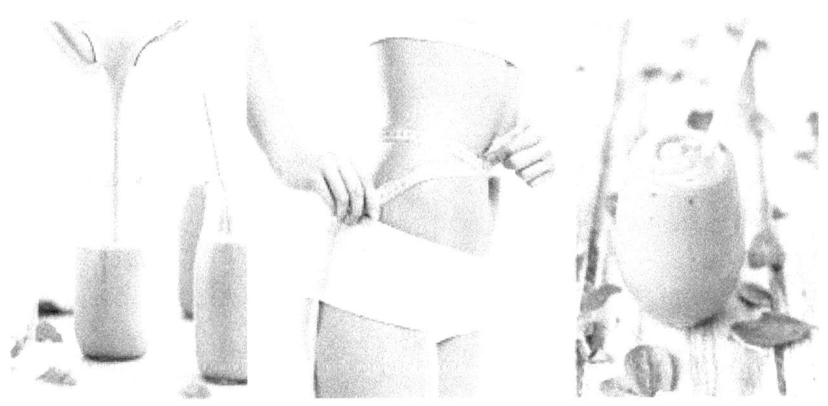

THIS PLAN REQUIRES a full cleanse, which means eating smoothies, snacks, and water for 7 days straight! This cleanse can help to adjust your body and push it to maintain a healthy eating habit.

The main guidelines you need to follow concerning what you should and should not eat.

What to Eat and Drink

✓ Green smoothies with raw vegetables only.

✓ Vegetables to eat: arugula, beet greens, Swiss chard, spinach, kale, lettuce, sorrel, carrot top leaves, parsley, and turnip and other.

✓ Fruits to eat: bananas, blueberries, apples, mango, peaches, strawberries, pineapple, lemon, limes, cherries, grapefruit, goji berries, cranberries, pears, kiwi, and papaya. Not use fruits that are not ripe.

✓ Drink water daily. 50 ounces (1.5 L) of water in a day, have three servings of your smoothies in a day. Drink spring or purified water.

✓ Prepare your green cleanse smoothie, because smoothies contain whole foods with fiber. You are using this smoothie as your source of food for the whole ten days, not a supplement, so it is important to blend the whole ingredients and not extract the juice instead.

✓ Sip on the smoothies, as you get hungry during the day about every three to four hours.

✓ Snacks can include carrot, cucumbers, apples, and crunchy vegetables like cabbage.

✓ Protein snacks like boiled egg and raw nuts are advised to be added as additional supplements.

✓ Drink a lot of water each day, as much as you can, or herbal teas.

What to Avoid

✓ Refined sugar or white sugar, which includes starchy vegetables, like sweet potato, and carrots must not be added to your smoothies.

✓ Fried meals because they have a high fat content, which is exactly what you do not need during this cleansing.

✓ Animal foods: dairy and meat

✓ Coffee, beer, liquor, soda, or even diet soda

THE 7-DAY GREEN SMOOTHIE CLEANSE PLAN

All you have to do is adhere to 7-day cleanse plan and you are steps away from achieving a slimmer, more healthy body.

DAY 1

Breakfast Smoothie: Peach and Spinach Green Smoothie

Lunch Smoothie: Broccoli and Blueberry Green Smoothie

Snack: 2 apples (diced) with 2 tbsp. almond butter

Dinner: Clean Greens Salad. Prepare a vinaigrette made with 2 tablespoons extra-virgin olive oil, 1 tablespoons lemon juice, and 1 tablespoon dried oregano. Combine 10 thinly sliced radishes, 1 cup mixed greens (lettuce, parsley), and ¼ thinly sliced red onion. Toss salad with dressing and top with ½ thinly sliced avocado.

DAY 2

Breakfast Smoothie: Vanilla Green Smoothie

Lunch Smoothie: Fruit and Lettuce Green Smoothie

Snack: 10 raw nuts, 1 carrot, 1 apple (diced)

Dinner: Slices of hard-boiled eggs, cooked salmon, and orange juice

DAY 3

Breakfast Smoothie: Banana Avocado Green Smoothie

Lunch Smoothie: Lime Banana Green Smoothie

Snack: ½ cup (150 g) raw nuts (almonds, pecans, cashew, walnut) for choice

Dinner: Brussels Sprout with Green Salad. Make dressing with 2 teaspoons honey, 3 tablespoons apple cider vinegar, 2 tablespoons extra-virgin olive oil, and ½ teaspoon sea salt. Toss dressing with 2 cups (160 g) thinly sliced Brussels sprouts, ¼ cup (35 g) dried cranberries, and ¼ cup (35 g) thinly sliced toasted almonds. Top with a grated cheese.

DAY 4

Breakfast Smoothie: Banana and Kiwi Green Smoothie

Lunch Smoothie: Mango Green Tea Smoothie

Snack: 1 green apple (diced), 10 raw nuts

Dinner: Green Roasted Spaghetti Squash: Roast 1 spaghetti squash in a 375-degree oven for 45 minutes or until fork-tender. Scrape out squash strands and serve with marinara sauce and a little Parmesan cheese.

DAY 5

Breakfast Smoothie: Ground Flax Seed Green Smoothie

Lunch Smoothie: Blueberry and Romaine Lettuce Green Smoothie

Snack: 1 ripe banana, ½ cup (100 g) fresh berries (for choice)

Dinner: Cleansing Cold Cucumber Soup. In a food processor, combine 1 large chopped cucumber, 1 ripe cubed avocado, 2 tablespoons chopped red onion, 1 tablespoon dill, juice of ½ lime, and 1 teaspoon sea salt. Blend for 30 seconds. Stream in 1 ½ cups (375

ml) cold water and blend until smooth. Chill for 30 minutes, or serve immediately and garnish with fresh dill sprigs.

DAY 6

Breakfast Smoothie: Kiwi Avocado Green Smoothie

Lunch Smoothie: Berry and Orange Juice Green Smoothie

Snack: 1 ripe banana (diced), 1 cup (200 g) fresh strawberries

Dinner: Avocado and Quinoa Salad. In a large salad bowl, combine 2 cups cooked and cooled quinoa, ¼ thinly sliced red onion, thinly sliced 1 green apple, and 2 cups (60 g) chopped kale leaves. Drizzle in juice of ½ lemon, 2 tablespoons extra-virgin olive oil, 2 teaspoons honey, and 1 pinch sea salt. Toss well. Gently fold in 1 cubed avocado and toss again.

DAY 7

Breakfast Smoothie: Basil Blueberry Green Smoothie

Lunch Smoothie: Pineapple and Avocado Green Smoothie

Snack: ½ ripe banana, 1 green apple, 1 kiwi, 10 almonds (all diced)

Dinner: Green Eggs with Gluten-Free Toast. Place gluten-free toast on 2 plates. Spread ½ tablespoon fresh pesto on each slice bread. Add thinly sliced tomato, avocado slices and 1 poached egg. Sprinkle with pepper and sea salt.

CHAPTER 2: GREEN SMOOTHIE RECIPES

SPINACH AND LETTUCE LEAVES SMOOTHIE

SERVINGS: 2 GLASSES

Cooking time: 10 minutes

Ingredients:

- 1 bunch of romaine lettuce
- 2 cups (60 g) raw spinach leaves
- 2 celery stalks
- 1 apple
- 1 pear
- 1 ripe banana

- ½ tbsp. fresh lemon juice
- 1 cup (250 ml) water

Cooking process:

1. Wash all vegetables, fruits and greens thoroughly before using them. Cut the greens. Peel the banana and cut into chunks. Remove the core and slice the apple and pear.
2. Put spinach, lettuce and water together in a blender. Blend at low speed until the mixture becomes smooth.
3. Add celery, apple and pear. Blend mass at high speed.
4. Add the banana, lemon juice, and mix until well blended. Pour in to glasses and serve fresh.

SPINACH AND COLLARD GREENS SMOOTHIE

SERVINGS: 1 GLASS

Cooking time: 10 minutes

Ingredients:

- 1 cup (30 g) spinach leaves
- 1 bunch of collard greens
- 4 whole oranges
- 2 cups (420 g) pineapple chunks

Cooking process:

1. Squeeze out the juice from the oranges. Use fresh juice as

liquid base for blending the greens together. Blend in the blender at slow speed until smooth.

2. Add the pineapples to the greens mass and blend at high speed until well mixed.
3. Pour and serve immediately.

MINTY PAPAYA GREEN SMOOTHIE

SERVINGS: 1 GLASS

Cooking time: 15 minutes

Ingredients:

- 3 cups (90 g) raw spinach leaves
- 1 ripe papaya
- 1 pear
- 2 tbsps. goji berries (dried or fresh)
- 12 fresh mint leaves
- 1 cup (250 ml) water

Cooking process:

1. Remove the core from the papaya and cut the pulp into cubes. Prepare the pear the same way. Wash and chop spinach.
2. Pour water into the blender. Add papaya, pear, goji and mint leaves. Add the spinach last.
3. Blend on high speed for about 30 seconds or until the smoothie turns into creamy consistency.
4. Pour into a glass and serve fresh.

GREEN PIÑA COLADA SMOOTHIE

SERVINGS: 4 GLASSES

Cooking time: 15 minutes

Ingredients:

- 1 cup (30 g) raw spinach leaves
- 3 cups (630 g) fresh ripe pineapple chunks
- ½ cup (50 g) shredded coconut core
- 5 dried pitted dates
- 2 cups (500 ml) unsweetened coconut water
- 1 cup ice cubes

Cooking process:

1. Put all the ingredients in a blender. Remember to put the liquid ingredients first and the greens last.
2. Blend on high speed until a creamy and smooth puree is achieved.
3. Pour in to glasses and serve.

BANANA AND KIWI GREEN SMOOTHIE

SERVINGS: 1 GLASS

Cooking time: 15 minutes

Ingredients:

- 1 bunch of kale
- 1 bunch of Romaine lettuce
- 1 bunch of Swiss chard leaves
- 1 ripe banana
- ½ kiwi
- ½ lemon
- 1 cup (250 ml) water

- 1 tsp. honey

Cooking process:

1. Wash all ingredients thoroughly. Chop all the greens. Peel and cut the banana and kiwi into chunks. Squeeze the lemon juice.
2. Put all the ingredients in a blender. Blend at high speed until smooth for 30 seconds.
3. Pour into a glass and serve immediately.

SPINACH AND MINT GREEN SMOOTHIE

SERVINGS: 2 GLASSES

Cooking time: 5 minutes

Ingredients:

- 1 cup (30 g) raw spinach leaves
- 10 mint leaves
- 4 whole pitted dates
- 2 tbsps. raw cashew butter
- 1 ½ cups (375 ml) water

Cooking process:

1. Put all the ingredients in a blender. Blend on high speed until smooth.
2. Pour in to glasses and serve immediately.

AVOCADO LIME CUCUMBER SMOOTHIE

SERVINGS: 1 GLASS

Cooking time: 15 minutes

Ingredients:

- 1 cup (30 g) raw spinach leaves
- 1 cucumber
- ½ avocado
- 3 whole limes
- 1 tsp. sweetener (to taste)
- 5 pieces ice cubes

Cooking process:

1. Wash vegetables, fruits and greens thoroughly.
2. Discard out the stems of spinach. Peel and quartered limes. Cut the cucumber into chunks. Remove the core from the avocado, slice the pulp.
3. In a blender, place cucumber, avocado, spinach and lime. Add ice cubes and the desired amount of sweetener.
4. Blend all ingredients until smooth for 1 minute. Pour into a glass and drink fresh.

KALE AVOCADO GREEN SMOOTHIE

SERVINGS: 1 GLASS

Cooking time: 15 minutes

Ingredients:

- ½ head of kale
- 1 medium sized apple
- 1 medium sized avocado
- ¼ lemon
- ½ tsp. ground ginger
- ½ cup (125 ml) water

Cooking process:

1. Rinse kale in running water. Tear leaves apart.
2. Peel and score an apple. Cut into cubes.
3. Cut avocado into halves, remove seed and scoop out the pulp using a tablespoon.
4. Peel lemon and remove seeds. Peel ginger and cut into thin slices.
5. Put all the ingredients in a blender. Blend on high speed until well mixed and smooth. Pour into a glass and enjoy!

SUMMER GREEN SMOOTHIE

SERVINGS: 2 GLASSES

Cooking time: 20 minutes

Ingredients:

- 8 mint leaves
- 8 basil leaves
- 8 coriander leaves
- 2 cups (300 g) diced watermelon chunks
- ½ small avocado
- 1 cucumber
- ½ lime
- ½ cup (125 ml) water

Cooking process:

1. Remove seeds from watermelon before cutting into chunks. Scoop out the pulp from the avocado. Squeeze the juice from the lime. Cut the cucumber into slices.
2. Put all the ingredients in a blender in this order: mint, basil, coriander, water, watermelon, avocado, cucumber, lime juice. Blend on high speed until smooth.
3. Pour into a glass and serve.

DETOX APPLE BROCCOLI SMOOTHIE

SERVINGS: 2 GLASSES

Cooking time: 15 minutes

Ingredients:

- 1 bunch of romaine lettuce
- ½ cup (88 g) broccoli florets
- 1 medium sized apple
- ½ orange
- ½ cup (125 ml) water
- 8 ice cubes

Cooking process:

1. Rinse greens and fruits under running water. Peel and core apple. Cut into 1-inch cubes.
2. Peel the orange. Remove seeds and separate into segments.
3. Put all the ingredients in a blender. Blend on high speed until thoroughly combined. Pour into a glass and serve.

FIG AND GINGER GREEN SMOOTHIE

SERVINGS: 1 GLASS

Cooking time: 15 minutes

Ingredients:

- 1 cup (30 g) raw spinach leaves
- 6 medium sized figs
- ½ tbsp. chopped ginger
- 3 whole pitted dates
- ½ cup (125 ml) water
- 1 cup ice cubes

Cooking process:

1. In a blender, add spinach and water. Blend until smooth.
2. Add all the remaining ingredients and process until blended smoothly. Pour into a glass and enjoy.

BANANA GREEN SMOOTHIE

SERVINGS: 1 GLASS

Cooking time: 15 minutes

Ingredients:

- ½ head of kale
- 2 ripe bananas
- ½ cup (125 ml) water
- 5 ice cubes

Cooking process:

1. Rinse kale in running water and clean thoroughly. Cut thinly.
2. Peel bananas and cut into slices.
3. Put all the ingredients in a blender and whiz until smooth. Pour into a glass and enjoy.

APPLE CUCUMBER GREEN SMOOTHIE

SERVINGS: 1 GLASS

Cooking time: 10 minutes

Ingredients:

- 1 green apple
- 1 ripe banana
- ½ cucumber
- 1 cup (250 ml) water

Cooking process:

1. Peel, core and cut apples into cubes. Peel the banana and cut into slices.
2. Without peeling, cut cucumbers into cubes.
3. Place all the ingredients in a blender and blend until smooth for 30 seconds. Pour into a glass and serve immediately.

CHOCOLATE GREEN SMOOTHIE

SERVINGS: 1 GLASS

Cooking time: 10 minutes

Ingredients:

- ½ head of kale
- ½ bunch of romaine lettuce
- ½ bunch of Swiss chard
- 1 ripe banana
- 1 tsp. unsweetened cacao powder
- 1 tbsp. natural honey
- 1 cup (250 ml) unsweetened coconut water

Cooking process:

1. Rinse and prepare greens and fruits. Chop the kale and lettuce leaves.
2. Peel the bananas and cut into slices.
3. Put all the ingredients in a blender and process until smooth. Pour into a glass and serve immediately.

DETOX GREEN SMOOTHIE

SERVINGS: 2 GLASSES

Cooking time: 15 minutes

Ingredients:

- ½ head of kale
- ½ cup (88 g) Brussels sprouts
- ½ cup (15 g) raw spinach leaves
- ½ avocado
- 1 medium sized green apple
- ½ cup (125 ml) water
- 5 ice cubes

Cooking process:

1. Wash and prepare the greens and fruits. Chop the kale leaves.
2. Scoop out the avocado pulp. Without peeling, core the apple and cut into cubes.
3. In a blender, mix kale, Brussels sprouts, spinach and water until smooth.
4. Add avocado, apple and ice cubes. Blend until smooth again.

MANGO CELERY SMOOTHIE

SERVINGS: 1 GLASS

Cooking time: 15 minutes

Ingredients:

- ½ head of kale
- ½ bunch of parsley
- 1 medium celery stalk
- ½ ripe mango
- 1 cup (250 ml) coconut water

Cooking process:

1. Wash and prepare greens and fruits.
2. Cut celery stalk into strips to facilitate easier blending. Chop the kale. Cut mango into big cubes.
3. Put all the ingredients in a blender and mix until smooth. Pour into a glass and enjoy.

FRUITY GREEN SMOOTHIE

SERVINGS: 1 GLASS

Cooking time: 15 minutes

Ingredients:

- ½ head of kale
- ½ cup (15 g) raw spinach leaves
- ½ cup (100 g) berries (raspberry or strawberry)
- 1 ripe banana
- 1 pear
- 1 cup (250 ml) water

Cooking process:

1. Peel and cut the banana into slices. Remove the seeds and cut the pear into cubes. Wash and chop the kale leaves.
2. Pour water; add kale and spinach in a blender. Blend until smooth for 1 minute.
3. Add the remaining ingredients and continue blending until smooth again.
4. Pour into a glass and serve immediately.

COCONUT GREEN SMOOTHIE

SERVINGS: 1 GLASS

Cooking time: 10 minutes

Ingredients:

- ½ head of kale
- 1 ripe banana
- 1 tsp. honey
- 1 cup (88 g) shredded coconut core
- 1 cup (250 ml) coconut water
- 5 ice cubes

Cooking process:

1. Peel and slice the banana.
2. In a blender, mix all the ingredients until smooth.
3. Pour into a glass and serve immediately.

BANANA AVOCADO GREEN SMOOTHIE

SERVINGS: 1 GLASS

Cooking time: 15 minutes

Ingredients:

- 1 cup (30 g) raw spinach leaves
- 1 bunch of Swiss chard leaves
- 1 ripe banana
- ½ medium sized cucumber
- ½ avocado
- 1 whole lime
- ½ cup (45 g) shredded coconut core
- 1 cup (250 ml) unsweetened coconut water

Cooking process:

1. Wash spinach, Swiss chard and cucumber thoroughly in running water. Chop the leaves and cut the cucumber into cubes.
2. Peel and slice the banana. Scoop out the pulp of the avocado. Peel and quarter the lime.
3. In a blender, mix spinach, Swiss chard and coconut water until smooth.
4. Add the remaining ingredients and mix thoroughly. Pour into a glass and enjoy.

KALE AND MANGO GREEN SMOOTHIE

SERVINGS: 1 GLASS

Cooking time: 15 minutes

Ingredients:

- 1 whole medium sized mango
- 1 head of kale
- 1 ripe banana
- ½ lime
- 1 cup (250 ml) unsweetened coconut milk

Cooking process:

1. Wash and prepare all the ingredients. Chop the kale leaves. Peel the mango, remove the seed and slice into cubes. Peel and cube banana. Juice the lime.
2. Pour coconut milk into the blender. Add mango, banana and lime juice. Add kale leaves last.
3. Blend all the ingredients on high speed until smoothie reaches a creamy consistency. Pour into a glass and serve fresh.

SPINACH YOGURT SMOOTHIE

SERVINGS: 2 GLASSES

Cooking time: 10 minutes

Ingredients:

- 1 cup (30 g) raw spinach leaves
- 1 whole orange
- 1 ripe banana
- ½ cup (100 g) strawberries
- ½ cup (125 ml) yogurt
- 10 ice cubes

Cooking process:

1. Peel oranges and divide into segments. Remove seeds. Peel and cube banana.
2. Put all the ingredients in a blender. Blend until smooth for 30 seconds.
3. Pour in to glasses and serve immediately.

LIME BANANA GREEN SMOOTHIE

SERVINGS: 1 GLASS

Cooking time: 10 minutes

Ingredients:

- 2 cups (60 g) raw spinach leaves
- 2 tbsps. lime juice
- 1 tsp. lime zest
- 1 ripe banana
- ¼ tsp. pure vanilla extract
- 1 whole pitted date
- 1 cup (250 ml) yogurt

Cooking process:

1. Wash greens and crushed. Peel and cube banana.
2. Put greens and fruit in a blender. Add liquid base and blend until smooth for 1 minute.
3. Pour into a tall glass and serve immediately.

TROPICAL GREEN SMOOTHIE

SERVINGS: 1 GLASS

Cooking time: 15 minutes

Ingredients:

- 2 cups (60 g) raw spinach leaves
- 1 ripe banana
- 1 ripe mango
- ⅓ cup (70 g) pineapple chunks
- ¼ cup (60 ml) orange juice

Cooking process:

1. Peel and cube the banana. Prepare the mango the same way. Wash the spinach.
2. Place the spinach, banana, mango, pineapple and orange juice in the blender. Blend for 1 minute until ingredients are mixed.
3. Pour into a glass and enjoy.

CARAMEL BANANA GREEN SMOOTHIE

SERVINGS: 2 GLASSES

Cooking time: 15 minutes

Ingredients:

- 1 cup (30 g) raw spinach leaves
- 1 ripe banana
- 1 tbsp. caramel
- 1 tbsp. raw walnuts
- ½ cup (125 ml) coconut milk
- ½ cup (125 ml) non-dairy milk (soy, oat, almond, hemp or rice)

Cooking process:

1. Peel and cube banana. Put spinach, coconut milk and non-dairy milk into a blender. Blend until thoroughly mixed.
2. Add banana, caramel and walnuts. Blend until smooth.
3. Pour into a tall glass and serve.

LINSEED MANGO GREEN SMOOTHIE

SERVINGS: 1 GLASS

Cooking time: 15 minutes

Ingredients:

- 1 cup (30 g) raw spinach leaves
- 1 ripe mango
- ½ tbsp. linseed
- 2 tbsps. desiccated coconut
- 2 tbsps. raisins
- ½ cup (125 ml) oat milk
- ½ cup (125 ml) water

Cooking process:

1. Remove the core and cube the pulp of mango. Blend spinach, oat milk and water together until mixed well.
2. Add mango, linseed, desiccated coconut and raisins and blend on high speed until mixture becomes smooth.
3. Pour into a tall glass and serve.

VANILLA AND ZUCCHINI GREEN SMOOTHIE

SERVINGS: 2 GLASSES

Cooking time: 15 minutes

Ingredients:

- 1 zucchini
- 1 cup (30 g) raw spinach leaves
- 1 small ripe banana
- 2 tbsps. pecan nuts
- 2 pitted dates
- 1 cup (250 ml) non-dairy milk
- ½ tsp. vanilla extract

Cooking process:

1. Wash the zucchini and spinach thoroughly. Without peeling, slice zucchini into half-inch thickness.
2. Peel the banana and cut into half-inch slices.
3. Put zucchini, spinach, vanilla extract and milk in a blender and process until smooth.
4. Add all the remaining ingredients and blend on high speed until smooth. Pour into a glass and drink.

SPINACH OAT GREEN SMOOTHIE

SERVINGS: 1 GLASS

Cooking time: 15 minutes

Ingredients:

- 1 cup (30 g) raw spinach leaves
- ½ cup (45 g) oats
- ½ tsp. vanilla extract
- ¼ cup (60 ml) unsweetened coconut milk
- 1 ½ cups (375 ml) water
- 5 ice cubes

Cooking process:

1. Blend spinach and water first.
2. When smooth, add oats, vanilla extract, coconut milk and ice cubes and blend until mixed.
3. Pour into a tall glass and serve.

PINEAPPLE COCONUT GREEN SMOOTHIE

SERVINGS: 1 GLASS

Cooking time: 10 minutes

Ingredients:

- 1 cup (30 g) raw spinach leaves
- 2 cups (420 g) pineapple chunks
- ¼ cup (60 ml) coconut milk
- ½ cup (125 ml) water
- 5 ice cubes

Cooking process:

1. Place all the ingredients in a blender. Blend until mixed thoroughly.
2. Pour into a glass and serve immediately.

FRUIT AND LETTUCE GREEN SMOOTHIE

SERVINGS: 2 GLASSES

Cooking time: 15 minutes

Ingredients:

- 1 bunch of romaine lettuce
- ½ cup (100 g) fresh strawberries
- ½ medium sized banana
- 1 apple
- 1 tbsp. ground flax seeds
- ½ cup (125 ml) non-dairy milk
- 5 ice cubes

Cooking process:

1. Remove the seeds from the apple and cut the pulp into chunks. Peel and cube banana. Chop the lettuce.
2. Blend lettuce, strawberries and milk until mixed thoroughly.
3. Add in banana, apple and flax seeds. Blend on high speed until smooth.
4. Blend in the ice cubes last. Pour into a tall glass and drink while cold.

VEGGIE AND GRAPEFRUIT GREEN SMOOTHIE

SERVINGS: 2 GLASSES

Cooking time: 15 minutes

Ingredients:

- ¼ cup (20 g) broccoli florets
- ¼ cup (20 g) cauliflower florets
- ½ pink grapefruit
- ½ tbsp. linseed
- ½ tbsp. almond nuts
- 2 pitted dates
- ½ cup (125 ml) non-dairy milk

- 1 cup (250 ml) water

Cooking process:

1. Peel and cube grapefruit.
2. Pour the water and milk in a blender. Add the broccoli, cauliflower and grapefruit. Blend until smooth.
3. Add linseed, almonds, and dates. Blend until smooth.
4. Pour into a tall glass and enjoy.

VANILLA GREEN SMOOTHIE

SERVINGS: 2 GLASSES

Cooking time: 15 minutes

Ingredients:

- 2 cups (60 g) raw spinach leaves
- 1 ½ (375 ml) cups freshly orange juice
- ¼ tsp. vanilla extract
- ½ cup (125 ml) almond milk
- 5 ice cubes

Cooking process:

1. Blend spinach, milk and water until smooth.

2. Add in the rest of the ingredients and continue blending for 1 minute.
3. Pour into tall glasses and serve immediately.

MANGO GREEN TEA SMOOTHIE

SERVINGS: 1 GLASS

Cooking time: 15 minutes

Ingredients:

- ½ cup (15 g) raw spinach leaves
- 1 ripe mango
- 1 tbsp. honey
- ½ cup(125 ml) freshly brewed green tea
- ½ cup (125 ml) low-fat yogurt
- 10 ice cubes

Cooking process:

1. Cool brewed green tea to room temperature.
2. Peel the mango, remove the core and slice.
3. In a blender, add spinach, yogurt and green tea. Blend until smooth for 30 seconds.
4. Add all remaining ingredients and process until smooth.
5. Pour into glasses and serve immediately.

PEACH AND YOGURT GREEN SMOOTHIE

SERVINGS: 1 GLASS

Cooking time: 15 minutes

Ingredients:

- 1 cup (30 g) raw spinach leaves
- 3 small whole peaches
- 1 tbsp. sesame seeds
- ½ cup (125 ml) almond milk
- ½ cup (125 ml) yogurt
- 5 ice cubes

Cooking process:

1. Blend in the spinach, milk and yogurt in a blender until smooth.
2. Pit peaches and cut into cubes.
3. Add all the remaining ingredients into a blender and mix until smooth.
4. Pour into a tall glass and drink immediately.

PISTACHIO KALE GREEN SMOOTHIE

SERVINGS: 2 GLASSES

Cooking time: 15 minutes

Ingredients:

- 1 head of kale
- 2 ripe bananas
- ½ cup (75 g) raw cashew
- 1 tbsp. maple syrup
- 1 tsp. vanilla extract
- ½ tsp. chopped ginger
- ½ cup (125 ml) water

- 20 ice cubes

Cooking process:

1. Peel and cube the bananas.
2. Put all the ingredients in a blender. Remember to put the liquid first and the greens last.
3. Blend on high speed until a creamy and smooth puree is achieved.
4. Pour in to glasses and serve.

STRAWBERRY AND OATS GREEN SMOOTHIE

SERVINGS: 1 GLASS

Cooking time: 10 minutes

Ingredients:

- 1 large celery stalk
- ½ cup (100 g) fresh strawberries
- 1 tsp. barley powder
- ½ cup (45 g) instant oats
- 1 tbsp. pumpkin seeds
- ½ cup (125 ml) oat milk
- ½ cup (125 ml) water

- 5 ice cubes

Cooking process:

1. Cut the celery into strips. Wash the berries.
2. Put celery, oats, ice cubes and water in a blender and whiz on high speed until smooth. Add strawberries, pumpkin seeds and milk and blend until smooth.
3. Pour into a tall glass and serve.

BROCCOLI AND BLUEBERRY GREEN SMOOTHIE

SERVINGS: 1 GLASS

Cooking time: 10 minutes

Ingredients:

- ½ cup (35 g) broccoli florets
- ½ cup (100 g) blueberries
- 1 ripe banana
- ½ cup (45 g) oats
- 1 tbsp. sunflower seeds
- ½ cup (125 ml) non-dairy milk to taste
- ½ cup (125 ml) water
- 5 ice cubes

Cooking process:

1. Peel and cube the banana. Put ice cubes, water, broccoli and oats in a blender. Blend on high speed until mixed.
2. Add milk, blueberries, bananas and sunflower seeds. Blend until smooth.
3. Pour into a glass and serve.

ORANGE STRAWBERRY GREEN SMOOTHIE

SERVINGS: 1 GLASS

Cooking time: 15 minutes

Ingredients:

- 1 cup (30 g) spinach leaves
- ¼ cup (60 ml) orange juice
- 2 cups (200 g) strawberries
- 1 tbsp. pecan nuts
- 5 pitted dates
- ½ cup (45 g) oats

- ½ tsp. vanilla extract
- ½ tsp. cinnamon
- ½ tsp. barley powder
- ¼ cup (60 ml) water

Cooking process:

1. Place water, orange juice, strawberries and spinach leaves in a blender. Blend until mixed thoroughly.
2. Next, add the rest of the ingredients. Blend until smooth.
3. Pour into a glass and serve.

MANGO AND MUESLI GREEN SMOOTHIE

SERVINGS: 1 GLASS

Cooking time: 15 minutes

Ingredients:

- ⅓ bunch of romaine lettuce
- 1 ripe mango
- 1 ripe banana
- ½ cup (45 g) muesli
- 1 tbsp. sesame seeds
- 5 pitted dates
- ½ cup (125 ml) non-dairy milk

- ½ cup (125 ml) water

Cooking process:

1. Peel and cube the banana. Remove the core and slice mango.
2. Place water, milk, muesli and lettuce in a blender. Mix thoroughly for 30 seconds.
3. Add the remaining ingredients and continue blending until smooth.
4. Pour into a glass and enjoy.

SPICY FRUIT GREEN SMOOTHIE

SERVINGS: 2 GLASSES

Cooking time: 10 minutes

Ingredients:

- 2 cups (60 g) raw spinach leaves
- 1 ripe banana
- ½ head of fresh pineapple
- 1 tbsp. lemon or lime juice
- ½ tsp. dried turmeric
- ⅓ tsp. dried ginger
- 1 tbsp. melted extra virgin coconut oil
- 1 cup (250 ml) water

Cooking process:

1. Peel and cube the banana. Peel and cube pineapple.
2. Add water, fresh spinach, banana cubes, pineapple cubes, lemon juice, turmeric and ginger to a blender. Blend in a high speed for 1 minute.
3. Slowly pour melted coconut oil. Blend for a couple more seconds. Try smoothie and adjust it to your liking. Pour into a glass.

GROUND FLAX SEED GREEN SMOOTHIE

SERVINGS: 2 GLASSES

Cooking time: 10 minutes

Ingredients:

- 1 head of kale
- 1 tbsp. ground flax seed
- 2 ripe bananas
- 1 ripe pear or apple
- ½ cup (125 ml) cold orange juice
- ½ cup (125 ml) cold water
- 10 ice cubes

Cooking process:

1. Peel and slice the banana. Remove the core and cube the pear or apple to taste.
2. Place bananas, pear (or apple), kale, orange juice, water, ice cubes and flax seed into a blender.
3. Blend for 30 seconds until smooth. Pour in to glasses.

BERRY GREEN SMOOTHIE

SERVINGS: 2 GLASSES

Cooking time: 15 minutes

Ingredients:

- 2 cups (60 g) raw spinach leaves
- 1 ripe banana
- ½ cup (100 g) blueberries
- ½ cup (100 g) raspberries
- 1 cup (100 g) pitted cherries
- 2 cups (250 ml) water

Cooking process:

1. Wash all the berries, cherries and spinach before using them.

Remove the pits from the cherries. Peel and cube the banana.

2. Add the water and the spinach to your blender. Blend until the mass is smooth.
3. Add the banana and continue blending. Last, place the berries in the blender and continue to blend until you have a smooth mixture. Pour smoothie two glasses and enjoy.

ORANGE AND FLAX SEED GREEN SMOOTHIE

SERVINGS: 2 GLASSES

Cooking time: 15 minutes

Ingredients:

- 2 cups (60 g) raw spinach leaves
- 1 medium-sized orange
- 2 cups (200 g) raspberries
- 1 ripe banana
- 2 tbsps. ground flax seeds
- 5 pitted dates
- 10 ice cubes

- 1 cup (250 ml) water

Cooking process:

1. Peel and cube the banana. Peel and divide the orange into pieces. Place all ingredients in the blender in the order listed. Add water to the blender.
2. Blend until completely smooth for 1 minute.
3. Pour into glasses and serve immediately.

GRAPEFRUIT KALE GREEN SMOOTHIE

SERVINGS: 2 GLASSES

Cooking time: 15 minutes

Ingredients:

- 1 head of kale
- ½ cucumber
- 1 medium apple
- 4 celery stalks
- 1 grapefruit
- 1 lime
- 1 cup (250 ml) water

Cooking process:

1. Core and peel the apple and remove the peel from the grapefruit and lime. Cut the apple into chunks. Cube the cucumber.
2. Place the kale, cucumber and the water into the blender, blending until smooth.
3. Add the celery and blend again. Add the apple pieces, grapefruit and lime to the blender. Continue mixing until smooth. Pour in to glasses.

BLUEBERRY AND ROMAINE LETTUCE GREEN SMOOTHIE

SERVINGS: 1 GLASS

Cooking time: 15 minutes

Ingredients:

- 1 head of romaine lettuce
- ¾ cup (140 g) blueberries
- 1 green apple
- ¼ lime
- 2 cups (250 ml) water

Cooking process:

1. Wash the apple and then chop it into chunks. Wash the

romaine lettuce and dry thoroughly. Peel the rind off the piece of lime.

2. Add the water to the blender and then place the romaine lettuce. Blend until the lettuce and water make a liquid mass.
3. Add the lime, apple chunks and the blueberries. Blend until the smoothie reaches your preferred consistency. Pour into glass and serve.

PEACH AND GRAPE GREEN SMOOTHIE

SERVINGS: 2 GLASSES

Cooking time: 15 minutes

Ingredients:

- 2 cups (60 g) raw spinach leaves
- 2 peaches
- 2 cups (200 g) green grapes
- 1 cup (250 ml) coconut water

Cooking process:

1. Wash the peaches, and then peel them and remove the pits. Wash the grapes and spinach as well.
2. Place the coconut water and fresh spinach in the blender, blending until smooth.
3. Add grapes and peaches and keep blending. If needed, add a bit more coconut water. Pour in to glasses.

ORANGE POMEGRANATE GREEN SMOOTHIE

SERVINGS: 2 GLASSES

Cooking time: 15 minutes

Ingredients:

- 2 cups (60 g) raw spinach leaves
- 1 ripe banana
- ¾ cup (180 ml) orange juice
- 1 cup (175 g) pomegranate seeds

- 1 ¼ cups (310 ml) water

Cooking process:

1. Peel the banana and wash the spinach. Remove the pomegranate seeds.
2. Add the water, orange juice and spinach to your blender. Blend until you smooth mass.
3. Add the banana chunks and pomegranate seeds to the blender. Continue blending until your smoothie is finished. Pour in to glasses.

CILANTRO AND ROMAINE LETTUCE GREEN SMOOTHIE

SERVINGS: 2 GLASSES

Cooking time: 20 minutes

Ingredients:

- ½ bunch of cilantro
- ½ bunch of romaine lettuce
- 2 celery stalks
- 1 cucumber
- ½ peeled lemon
- ½ jalapeno
- 1 inch piece of fresh ginger

- 1 cup (250 ml) water

Cooking process:

1. Wash all of the veggies. Cut the cucumber, celery stalks and ginger into chunks. Chop the jalapeno. Chopped greens.
2. Add the water, cilantro and romaine lettuce to your blender. Blend until smooth.
3. Add the lemon, celery, cucumber, jalapeno and ginger. Continue blending. Add more water if the mass is too thick. Pour in to glasses and serve.

BANANA ROMAINE LETTUCE GREEN SMOOTHIE

SERVINGS: 4 GLASSES

Cooking time: 20 minutes

Ingredients:

- 1 bunch of romaine lettuce
- 3 stalks celery
- ⅓ bunch of fresh cilantro
- ⅓ bunch of fresh parsley
- 1 ripe banana
- 2 green apples

- ½ fresh lemon
- 1 ½ cups (375 ml) cold water

Cooking process:

1. Peel the banana and cut into chunks. Wash and chop the romaine, parsley and cilantro. Cut the celery into chunks.
2. Juice the ½ lemon and reserve juice. Wash the apple and then remove the core. Chop the apple into pieces.
3. In the blender, combine the romaine lettuce, parsley, cilantro and water. Blend on low until smooth.
4. Add the apples and celery; increase the blending speed.
5. Last, add the lemon juice and banana chunks, continuing to blend until the entire mass is smooth. Pour in to glasses.

KIWI AVOCADO GREEN SMOOTHIE

SERVINGS: 2 GLASSES

Cooking time: 15 minutes

Ingredients:

- 2 cups (60 g) raw spinach leaves
- ½ avocado
- 1 kiwi
- 1 banana
- 1 cup (200 g) blueberries
- 1 cup (200 g) raspberries or strawberries
- 2 cups (500 ml) water

Cooking process:

1. Wash the spinach and the berries. Peel the banana and then chop into big chunks.
2. Cut an avocado in half, use the side that does not have the core and chop. Wash and chop the kiwi.
3. Blend the spinach and the water together in your blender until smooth.
4. Add the kiwi, avocado, blueberries, raspberries and banana chunks to the blender. Continue blending until smooth. Pour in to glasses.

PEACH AND SPINACH GREEN SMOOTHIE

SERVINGS: 2 GLASSES

Cooking time: 15 minutes

Ingredients:

- 2 cups (60 g) raw spinach leaves
- 1 cup (250 ml) fresh squeezed orange juice
- 2 peaches
- ½ cup (125 ml) cold water

Cooking process:

1. Wash the spinach leaves and set to the side to dry. Wash peaches. Peel the peaches and remove the pits. Chop the peaches into pieces.
2. In the blender, mix the water, orange juice and the spinach leaves until smooth.
3. Once the mixture is smooth, add the peach pieces to the blender. Keep blending until smooth. Pour in to glasses.

PINEAPPLE AND LETTUCE GREEN SMOOTHIE

SERVINGS: 1 GLASS

Cooking time: 15 minutes

Ingredients:

- ½ bunch of parsley
- 1 bunch of lettuce leaves
- ½ head of kale
- ½ pineapple
- ½ ripe banana
- 1 cup (250 ml) cold water

Cooking process:

1. Peel and chop banana. Wash and chop them. Chop the pineapple into chunks. Wash the parsley and lettuce leaves.
2. Add the water, kale, lettuce and parsley to your blender. Blend on low until the greens combine with the water, creating a smooth mass.
3. Add banana and pineapple chunks to your blender. Increase the speed and continue blending. Pour the smoothie in a glass and enjoy.

MANGO BANANA GREEN SMOOTHIE

SERVINGS: 1 GLASS

Cooking time: 10 minutes

Ingredients:

- 2 large mangoes
- 1 medium-sized ripe banana
- 2 cups (60 g) raw spinach leaves
- 1 cup (250 ml) water

Cooking process:

1. Peel the mangoes and then chop them into medium-sized pieces. Peel the banana and chop. Wash the spinach.
2. Place water and spinach leaves in your blender, blending at low speed until smooth.
3. Add banana and mango. Increase blender speed and keep blending until the mixture reaches smoothie consistency. Pout into glass and serve.

ROMAINE LETTUCE GRAPE GREEN SMOOTHIE

SERVINGS: 1 GLASS

Cooking time: 15 minutes

Ingredients:

- ½ bunch of romaine lettuce
- 1 cup (100 g) seedless red grapes
- 1 ripe banana
- 1 cup (200 g) strawberries

Cooking process:

1. Wash the grapes and the romaine lettuce. Peel and chop the banana ahead of time, placing the chunks.
2. Place the grapes in a blender. Blend until the grapes start creating a liquid.
3. Add the romaine lettuce and continue blending. If needed, add a little water.
4. Add the strawberries and banana pieces. Continue blending until you have a thick smoothie. Pour into glass and serve.

FLAX SEED AND BERRY GREEN SMOOTHIE

SERVINGS: 2 GLASSES

Cooking time: 15 minutes

Ingredients:

- 2 cups (60 g) raw spinach leaves
- 1 green apple
- ½ cup (50 g) seedless grapes
- ½ mango
- 1 cup (200 g) strawberries
- 1 cup (250 ml) water
- 2 tbsps. flax seed

Cooking process:

1. Wash the apple, grapes, mango and spinach leaves. Remove the core and chop the apple into pieces. Remove the peel from the mango and then chop into pieces.
2. Place water, the flax seed and the spinach leaves into your blender and start blending at low speed until smooth.
3. Add in the apple chunks, grapes, mango chunks, and strawberries. Keep blending, increasing the blender speed until your mixture is nice and smooth. Pour in to glasses.

GINGER CILANTRO LIME GREEN SMOOTHIE

SERVINGS: 2 GLASSES

Cooking time: 15 minutes

Ingredients:

- 1 ½ cups (45 g) raw spinach leaves
- ½ bunch of cilantro
- 1 inch of fresh ginger
- 1 lime
- 3 ripe bananas

- 2 cups (500 ml) water

Cooking process:

1. Wash the spinach leaves and cilantro. Peel the lime and remove the seeds from the lime. Wash ginger and cut into pieces. Peel the bananas and then cut them into chunks.
2. Pour water to the blender and then add the spinach leaves and the cilantro. Start blending at low speed until it turns into a liquid.
3. Add the lime, bananas and ginger to the blender and start blending again at low speed. Slowly increase the speed and blend until the smoothie reaches the consistency you want. Pour in to glasses.

ARUGULA STRAWBERRY GREEN SMOOTHIE

SERVINGS: 2 GLASSES

Cooking time: 20 minutes

Ingredients:

- 1 cup (30 g) raw spinach leaves
- 1 cup (20 g) arugula
- 1 bunch of romaine lettuce
- 2 green apples
- 1 ripe banana

- 1 ½ cups (250 g) strawberries
- 2 tbsps. flax seed
- 2 cups (500 ml) water

Cooking process:

1. Wash the apples and core them. Cut the apples into chunks. Wash the spinach, arugula and romaine lettuce. Peel the banana and cut it into chunks.
2. Pour the water into the blender. Add the spinach, arugula and romaine. Begin blending at low speed. Continue until the greens blend with the water to become smooth.
3. Place the flax seed, apple chunks, banana chunks, and strawberries into the blender. Start blending at slow speed again. Increase the speed as necessary. Pour in to glasses.

BERRY AND ORANGE JUICE GREEN SMOOTHIE

SERVINGS: 2 GLASSES

Cooking time: 20 minutes

Ingredients:

- 2 cups (60 g) raw spinach leaves
- ¾ cup (180 ml) squeezed orange juice
- 1 cup (200 g) blueberries
- 1 cup (200 g) raspberries

- 2 medium ripe bananas
- ½ tsp. chia seeds
- ¾ cup (180 ml) water

Cooking process:

1. Wash the spinach leaves. Peel the bananas and then cut them into chunks.
2. Pour the purified water and the orange juice into your blender.
3. Add the spinach leaves and start blending at low speed. Continue until your mixture is smooth.
4. Add the blueberries, raspberries and the chunks of banana. Start slow and then increase the speed. Stop when you reach the consistency that you want for your smoothie. Pour in to glasses and sprinkle with chia seeds.

MANGO GINGER GREEN SMOOTHIE

SERVINGS: 2 GLASSES

Cooking time: 15 minutes

Ingredients:

- 1 cup (30 g) raw spinach leaves
- 1 bunch of fresh parsley
- 2 celery sticks
- 1 lemon
- 1 cucumber
- 1 mango
- 1 tsp. chopped fresh ginger

- 2 cups (500 ml) water

Cooking process:

1. Wash the parsley, celery, cucumber and spinach leaves. Cut the celery and cucumber into chunks to make them easier to blend. Peel the lemon and remove its seeds. Chop the mango into chunks.
2. Pour the water into the blender. Add the parsley, celery chunks, cucumber chunks and the spinach leaves. Start blending until your mixture becomes smooth.
3. Place the mango chunks, lemon and ginger into the blender. Begin blending again, increasing the speed until the mass becomes smooth. Serve immediately and enjoy.

SPINACH AND COCONUT GREEN SMOOTHIE

SERVINGS: 1 GLASS

Cooking time: 10 minutes

Ingredients:

- 3 cups (90 g) raw spinach leaves
- 1 whole coconut

Cooking process:

1. Wash the spinach and set to the side.
2. To open the coconut, start by opening it using a cleaver. Pour the water out of the coconut, right into your blender. Then, use a spoon to dig out the coconut meat, adding it to the blender too. Blend the coconut water and coconut meat together until it is smooth.
3. Add the reserved spinach to the blender. Start blending on low, increasing speed slowly until the mixture becomes smooth. Pour into a glass and enjoy.

PEACH AND BERRY GREEN SMOOTHIE

SERVINGS: 2 GLASSES

Cooking time: 15 minutes

Ingredients:

- 1 cup (30 g) raw spinach leaves
- 1 head of kale
- 1 large peach
- 1 ½ cups (250 g) mixed berries
- 1 green apple

- 2 cups (250 ml) water
- 1 tbsp. flax seed
- 1 tsp. protein powder for choice
- 2 tsps. stevia

Cooking process:

1. Wash an apple, remove the core and cut into chunks. Wash the peach, remove the pit and cut it up. Wash the spinach and kale, chopping the kale into smaller pieces.
2. Pour the water into the blender. Add chopped kale and the fresh spinach leaves. Begin blending.
3. Once you have a smooth mixture, add the apple chunks, flax seed, peach pieces, mixed berries, protein powder and stevia. Continue blending until the mixture reaches your desired thickness. Pour in to glasses.

PINEAPPLE AND AVOCADO GREEN SMOOTHIE

SERVINGS: 2 GLASSES

Cooking time: 15 minutes

Ingredients:

- 2 cups (60 g) raw spinach leaves
- 1 ripe avocado
- 2 cups (420 g) pineapple chunks
- 2 cups (500 ml) coconut water

Cooking process:

1. Remove the seed from the avocado and scoop out the pulp. Wash the spinach leaves before using them.
2. Pour the coconut water into the blender and then add your spinach leaves. Turn the blender on low and blend until the spinach and water make a smooth liquid.
3. Add in the avocado and the pineapple. Continue blending, allowing blending until you have the thickness you desire from your green smoothie. Pour in to glasses.

ALMOND AND BERRY GREEN SMOOTHIE

SERVINGS: 2 GLASSES

Cooking time: 15 minutes

Ingredients:

- 2 cups (60 g) raw spinach leaves
- 1 medium ripe banana
- ½ cup (65 g) pre-soaked raw almonds
- 1 cup (200 g) blueberries

- 1 cup (200 g) strawberries
- 2 cups (500 ml) unsweetened almond milk

Cooking process:

1. Wash the spinach leaves and then peel the banana. Cut the banana into chunks.
2. Blend the spinach and the almond milk in the blender until you have a smooth.
3. Once the mixture is smooth, add the banana chunks, almonds, blueberries and strawberries. Start blending again. Continue, increasing the speed of the blender until you have the desired thickness for your green smoothie. Pour in to glasses.

BASIL BLUEBERRY GREEN SMOOTHIE

SERVINGS: 4 GLASSES

Cooking time: 15 minutes

Ingredients:

- 15 basil leaves
- 1 bunch of fresh parsley
- ½ avocado
- ½ cucumber
- 1 ripe banana
- ¾ cup (140 g) blueberries
- 2 cups (500 ml) water

- ½ lemon
- 3-4 ice cubes

Cooking process:

1. Wash the basil, parsley and cucumber. Leave the skin on the cucumber and cut into chunks. Peel the banana and then cut into slices. Juice the lemon and set juice to the side. Scoop out the avocado.
2. Pour the water and lemon juice into the blender. Add the basil leaves and the parsley. Start blending at low speed. Blend until you have a thick, smooth mixture.
3. Add the banana, ice cubes, cucumber, blueberries, and avocado to the blender. Start blending again, increasing the speed if necessary.
4. Stop when the smoothie reaches the consistency you desire. Pour in to glasses.

SPIRULINA GINGER GREEN SMOOTHIE

SERVINGS: 1 GLASS

Cooking time: 10 minutes

Ingredients:

- 1 tsp. spirulina
- ½ tsp. ground ginger
- 1 cup (30 g) raw spinach leaves
- 1 cup (250 ml) fruit yogurt

Cooking process:

1. Place the spirulina with the spinach leaves in the blender and mix until smooth.
2. Add the fruit yogurt and ground ginger. Mix again on high speed for 30 seconds. Pour into glass and serve.

APPLE PINEAPPLE GREEN SMOOTHIE

SERVINGS: 1 GLASS

Cooking time: 10 minutes

Ingredients:

- 1 head of lettuce leaves
- 1 stalk celery
- 2 green apples
- 2 cups (420 g) cubed pineapple
- 1 cup (250 ml) almond milk

Cooking process:

1. Peel and cube apples. Wash greens and chop.
2. Add all the ingredients except the greens in your blender.

1. Blend on high speed for 30 seconds.
2. Add the greens and blend on high until the smoothie is creamy. Pour into a glass and serve.

SPINACH AND LETTUCE GREEN SMOOTHIE

SERVINGS: 2 GLASSES

Cooking time: 15 minutes

Ingredients:

- 1 bunch of romaine lettuce
- 2 cups (60 g) raw spinach leaves
- 2 celery stalks
- 1 green apple

- 1 pear
- 1 ripe banana
- ½ tbsp. lemon juice
- 1 cup (250 ml) water

Cooking process:

1. Wash all vegetables and fruits thoroughly before using them. Cut the greens. Remove the core of apple and pear, cut them into chunks. Peel and cubed banana.
2. Put romaine lettuce, spinach and water together in a blender. Process at low speed until the mixture becomes smooth.
3. Add celery, apple and pear. Blend mixture at high speed.
4. Lastly, add the banana and lemon juice, mix again until smooth. Pour in to glasses and serve fresh.

SPINACH AND COLLARD SMOOTHIE

SERVINGS: 1 GLASS

Cooking time: 10 minutes

Ingredients:

- 1 cup (30 g) raw spinach leaves
- 1 bunch of fresh collard greens
- 4 whole medium sized oranges
- 3 cups (630 g) pineapple chunks

Cooking process:

1. Squeeze out the juice from the oranges. Use this fresh juice as liquid base. Place spinach, collard greens in the blender. Pour the juice, blend at slow speed until smooth.
2. Add the pineapples to the orange and greens mixture and blend at high speed until well mixed.
3. Pour and serve immediately.

AVOCADO LIME GREEN SMOOTHIE

SERVINGS: 1 GLASS

Cooking time: 15 minutes

Ingredients:

- 1 cup (30 g) raw spinach leaves
- 1 cucumber
- ½ avocado
- 3 whole limes
- 1 tsp. sweetener (honey, agave or stevia) to taste
- 5 ice cubes

Cooking process:

1. Wash vegetables and fruits thoroughly. Cut the leaves of the spinach. Without peeling, cut cucumber into half-inch slices.
2. Remove seed of avocado. Using a spoon, scoop out the flesh from the peeling. Peel and cut into quarters lime.
3. In a blender, place cucumber, avocado, spinach and lime. Add ice cubes and the desired amount of sweetener.
4. Blend all ingredients until smooth. Pour into a glass and drink fresh.

POMEGRANATE FRUITS GREEN SMOOTHIE

SERVINGS: 2 GLASSES

Cooking time: 20 minutes

Ingredients:

- 2 cups (60 g) raw spinach leaves
- 1 stalk celery
- 1 cup (175 g) pomegranate seeds
- 5 strawberries
- 1 red apple
- 1 peach
- ½ cup (50 g) red grapes
- 1 ripe banana
- 1 cup (250 ml) water

Cooking process:

1. Wash the greens and chop them.
2. Wash all the fruits. Remove the core of apple and peach, cut them into chunks. Peel and chop banana.
3. Place greens in blender and pour the water. Blend at high speed for 30 seconds.
4. Add other ingredients. Continue to blend for another 30 seconds. Pour in to glasses and serve.

FRUITS AND SEEDS GREEN SMOOTHIE

SERVINGS: 1 GLASS

Cooking time: 15 minutes

Ingredients:

- 1 head of kale
- 1 tsp. spirulina powder
- 1 tbsp. chia seeds
- 1 tbsp. hemp seeds
- 1 ripe banana
- ½ cup (210 g) pineapple chunks
- 1 mango
- ¾ cup (180 ml) orange juice

Cooking process:

1. Wash and chop kale leaves. Peel and cut banana into chunks. Remove the core from the mango, and then cut into chunks.
2. Place the ingredients, except for the hemp seeds, in a blender and blend until smooth.
3. Pour into a glass and sprinkle with hemp seeds.

CONCLUSION

To be trim does not necessarily mean depriving yourself of essential nutrients and the joy of eating. You need just reduce your caloric intake, but take in nutritious, satisfying and delicious foods. The journey to weight loss can be done with green smoothies that will keep you healthy.

DRINKING GREEN SMOOTHIE regularly can help you protect optimum health. This is a powerful tool for shedding pounds, strengthening your immune system, ending food cravings and bringing about a general sense of better well-being.

This green smoothie recipe book helps you get on to your healthy journey.

Just to reiterate some of the most important things we have covered, here is a quick list:

✓ Use only fresh organic fruit

✓ Wash your produce thoroughly before using it

✓ Drink your smoothie immediately after cooking

✓ Eliminate bad habits such as smoking, drinking caffeine, or consuming large amounts of sugar at least two weeks prior to a cleanse

Keep using the green smoothie recipes in this book, even after you finish the 7-day cleanse. You will continue to reap all the benefits smoothies have to offer and changing your lifestyle will result in a healthier body.

The road to a healthy you is fast and easy with green smoothies!

www.ingramcontent.com/pod-product-compliance
Ingram Content Group UK Ltd.
Pitfield, Milton Keynes, MK11 3LW, UK
UKHW021932200726
13853UKWH00010B/359